CORNISH
MOODS

Oliver Hawker

HALSGROVE

First published in Great Britain in 2003

Copyright © 2003 Oliver Hawker

Title page photograph: **Porth Nanven Looking to the Brisons**

Large prints of selected images from this book are available at
www.ebbtidegallery.com or phone: **01736 787862**

British Library Cataloguing-in-Publication Data
A CIP record for this title is available from the British Library

ISBN 1 84114 263 8

HALSGROVE
Halsgrove House
Lower Moor Way
Tiverton, Devon EX16 6SS
Tel: 01884 243242
Fax: 01884 243325
email: sales@halsgrove.com
website: www.halsgrove.com

Printed and bound in Spain

INTRODUCTION

Devon may be pretty, but Cornwall is 'andsome. The first and last county in Britain possesses a timeless feel that is quite unlike anywhere else in the country. Walking around Cornwall's harbour villages, or across its sandy beaches, or over its windswept moors, you may easily forget that you are still in England; the Cornish you meet along the way may well inform you that you are indeed *not* in England.

When the sun shines in the summer, Cornwall has no equal in Europe. The countries of the Iberian peninsula may also boast the emerald sea that sparkles under a crystal sky, and the light golden sands that shimmer through the heat haze, but they don't have lush green fields lying immediately behind them, sectioned by hedges brimming with biota jostling for an anchor on the ancient stone walls that support them. The Greek islands may well have the same rocky inlets which hide deep-green lagoons where you can wade through the water for half a mile without getting your shoulders wet, but with them comes a hot oppressive breeze that makes lazing on the beach a test of stamina. There are no dense deciduous woods that nestle in stream-worn valleys, holding the moisture to cool a heavy head. Indeed the towns and cities of France and Italy have their share of antiquities, but they are always viewed through a film of smog as the prevailing easterly winds in those parts bring with them 5000-miles' worth of dry dust and petrol fumes. The air in Cornwall, purified by the Atlantic, is as clean as you can possibly get, and lends a sharpness, a clarity, to everything around you, and allows lichens to flourish on every available perch, rock, tree branch and rooftop, adding yet more colour to the scene.

The autumn brings its own marvels. From late August through to November, as the moors and cliff tops explode into purple, the heath is heralding the end of time of plenty and forewarning of harder times to come. The wind, that for months has caressed the coastal waters and served to cool the bathers on the beaches, now charges itself for an onslaught. Around mid-October it veers, oh so slightly, from a southerly to a south-westerly, and begins to blow with the force of the Devil, provoking the seas into a frenzied attack on the granite fortress that is the far west. Boulders as big as a man are scooped up from the seabed, and propelled, like cannon balls at the cliffs; the ocean becomes as a ham-fisted sculptor let loose on ancient stone. Yet down here December days can be as temperate as any day in April or May. When the gales have exhausted themselves for a while, and the sun peeps through the mists, you could easily be fooled into thinking that spring is just around the corner. But January and February brood mean and wet, as wave after wave of Atlantic fronts lash the moors and coves; hillside streams that were but trickles in the high summer swell into a deluge that bursts through field boundaries, coalescing into rivers that charge down those roads that have been built by man on the ancients flood routes. The wintertime in Cornwall can be hard.

Cornwall has many faces, and the photographs in this book will reflect, I hope, the mercurial qualities of this fascinating county, and serve to evoke memories in years to come of your time here. Or if, like me, you are fortunate enough to call the county home, may this book remind you of the stunning beauty that surrounds you and encourage you to enjoy it while you can.

OLIVER HAWKER
JANUARY 2003

PICTURE LOCATIONS

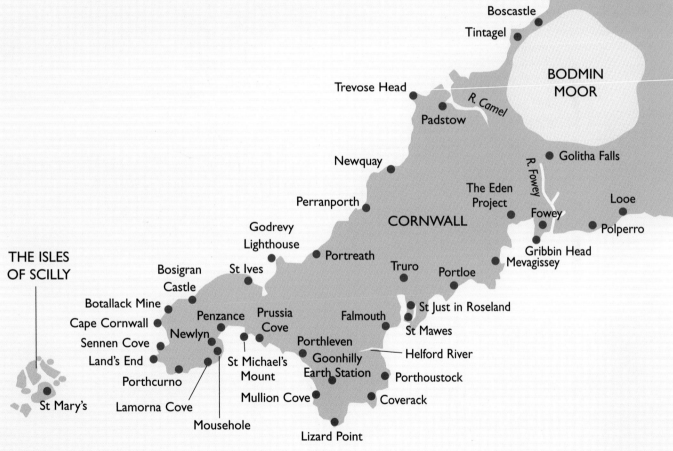

Boscastle
Tintagel
BODMIN MOOR
Trevose Head
R. Camel
Padstow
Newquay
Golitha Falls
R. Fowey
Perranporth
The Eden Project
Looe
CORNWALL
Fowey
Polperro
Godrevy Lighthouse
Gribbin Head
Mevagissey
THE ISLES OF SCILLY
St Ives
Portreath
Truro
Portloe
Bosigran Castle
Botallack Mine
St Just in Roseland
Cape Cornwall
Penzance
Prussia Cove
Falmouth
Newlyn
St Mawes
Sennen Cove
Porthleven
Helford River
Land's End
St Michael's Mount
Goonhilly Earth Station
Porthcurno
Porthoustock
St Mary's
Lamorna Cove
Mullion Cove
Coverack
Mousehole
Lizard Point

Harbour Reaches
Disturbed by walkers, a large flock of seagulls takes to the air over a very low tide in St Ives.

West Looe
The first breath of sunshine washes over the dwellings of this popular fishing town.

The Old Lookout
The crisp whiteness of this unusual building
at Willapark, near Boscastle, contrasts nicely with
the deep blue of the late-afternoon sky.

Bathing Huts, Porthgwidden
An incoming tide laps at this small but popular beach at St Ives.

Whitened Ruin
This old pile stands starkly against the snow in the fields around Botallack.

Dawn in the Marina, Penzance
The first light of day reveals the boats stranded by the low tide.

Opposite:
Sunset behind the Brisons
Here the famous offshore stacks serve to point the way to the end of the day.
Their size is dwarfed by an immense sky.

The Tate, St Ives
The interesting contours of this handsome art
gallery are repeated inside, and provide a suitably
photogenic setting for some fine exhibits.

Inland from Willapark
The moors and fields of the north-west are reminiscent of the Hampshire Downs.

Sunset Behind the Old Calciner, Botallack
Thrown into shadow, otherwise ugly ruins make an attractive frame for the end of another day.

A Sea of Yellow
This field of chrysanthemums contrasts beautifully
with the deep-blue sky of a hot afternoon.

Inland from Cape Cornwall
The rusty colours of autumn are enhanced by the late-afternoon light cast from a cloudless sky.

Opposite:
A Granite World
A tiny seated figure just visible in the crevice, top left, gives some perspective
on the scale of these wind-worn hulks of rock.

Golowan Festival Fireworks
Midsummer in Penzance is celebrated
in spectacular style.

St Just in Roseland
This sleepy backwater has given shelter to all manner of craft over the centuries.

The Most Southerly Breakers in Britain
Guillemots huddle on a rock as the swell boils around them.

The Reed Cutters
Demand for thatch is high in Cornwall, especially now that more and more houses are being renovated in the traditional way. These two men make the most of a sunny January afternoon.

The Enys Dodnan and Armed Knight, Land's End
Late-afternoon light softens the edges of these two granite stacks.

Opposite:
Portheras
The light-golden beaches in the far west – many comprising only crushed seashells –
reflect the light in such a way that the shallow waters at mid-tide appear a perfect aquamarine.

Polperro
This mix of working and pleasure craft reflects how
the lifestyles of the folk living in this popular
fishing village have changed over the years.

The Armed Knight
A closer look at this granite mass, taking its customary pounding.

China Cockerel
This bird peers out from a freshly painted window, which is pleasingly set off by grey slate.

Smugglers Cottage
A cat this time watches curiously from the window of this rustic house that overlooks Prussia Cove.

Evening at Nanven
The jostling sea is softened into a ghostly mist by the
long camera exposure required for this time of day.

Rainbow over the Dunes, Sennen Cove
As a rainbow follows in the wake of a sudden summer downpour,
the illuminated clifftop house promises that sunshine is on its way.

Opposite
Dawn, Newlyn
The lower edges of these clouds are scorched red by the rising sun which glows just below the horizon.

Looking to Porthmeor
The views from Carn Galver in West Penwith are among the most breathtaking in Cornwall.

Ponies on Bodmin
The rays of low afternoon catch the manes of these
ponies, huddling together in a biting wind.

High Moors Pony
This tethered pony braves all weathers throughout
the year. Here he enjoys a balmy June evening.

Winter Moors
A sudden covering of snow halts all activity on
the moors above Penzance. The salt air makes
sure it doesn't hang around for long, however.

Caressing Waves
The calm waters stroke the granite rocks exposed on the beach at Gwynver.

Rock Perch
Seagulls take a break during an incoming tide, at the entrance to the
tiny fishing port of Portloe on the Roseland peninsula.

Bosigran Castle
The sheer cliffs of this ancient defensive stronghold proved impregnable to invaders.

Menhir
Standing stones have withstood the elements
for thousands of years. How many sunsets has
this particular one witnessed?

Across Padstow Bay
From Cat's Cove the view leads all the way to Pentire Point.

Wheal Bal in the Snow
A sudden cold snap leaves this old engine house standing
in stark contrast to the surrounding countryside.

House Line on the Harbour, Porthleven
A shaft of sun on a dour afternoon throws the foreground into vivid relief, against a threatening sky.

The Daymark at Gribbin Head
This smartly maintained antique colossus still serves as a valuable shipping aid
to pleasure craft travelling to and from Fowey and the surrounding harbours.

Monument, Carn Brea
This massive granite cross was erected in 1836 in honour of Lord
Francis Basset de Dunstanville, 'friend to the miners'.

Chûn Quoit
Another Cornish icon. Quoits and other ancient constructions abound
in the county, and make very photogenic subjects indeed.

Penzance Promenade
The calm waters of Mount's Bay lap gently against the harbour wall on a morning that gave way to a sizzling July day.

Carn Brea Castle
Another day dawns over this fourteenth-century outpost.
In the background the town of Redruth soaks up the morning sun.

Bare Tree overlooking the Helford River.

Dusky Purples
The low-contrast light that prevails for a few minutes after sunset can create some subtle nuances in colour.

The Hayle Towans
These massive sand dunes flank the mouth of the Hayle estuary.
On the St Ives' side they have been sculpted into a links golf course.

St Ives Bay Surfer
This lucky chap takes advantage of
some particularly fine conditions.

The Concentrating Surfer
Catching the smaller waves
can be harder than you think…

Done Surfin'
The swell abates. Time for our surfer to head home.

Plain-an-Gwary, St Just
Evening sunshine is the only lighting effect for this old amphitheatre. The grass banks
in the background provide equally simple seating for the audience during a performance.

Looking to Tater-du Lighthouse
Painted brilliant white, the lighthouse tower stands proud from brown granite cliffs and the gunmetal grey of the sea.

Trevalga Church
Sheep graze their way across the pasture land lying outside the village of Trevalga, near Boscastle.

Opposite:
The Whirlpool
The long exposure required for this shot highlights the behaviour
of the waves in this tiny cove, and shows that it is aptly named.

Irresistible Force Meets Immovable Object
And the results are awesome, seen here at Mousehole.

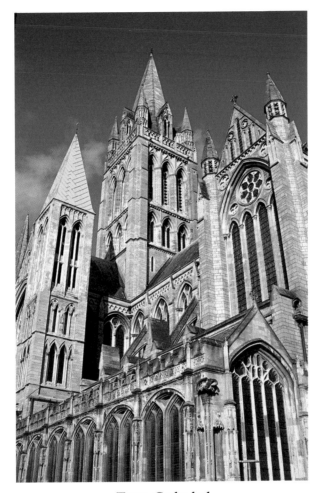

Truro Cathedral
This magnificent edifice is a relatively modern
addition to the Truro skyline and is the tallest
building in Cornwall.

Pendeen Watch
Guiding ships for over a hundred years, this proud sentinel is once again set for duty as the day bids its farewell.

Full Sail
Flying the flag of St Piran, this little pride and joy glides gently into Newlyn Harbour.

Freezing Coastline
All is still on the cliffs of the north coast as a rare icy blast lays siege to the county.

The Docks at Penzance
The crane silhouetted against an early light shows that the docks never rest, as boats load and offload twenty-four hours a day.

Bluebells, Blue Sea, Blue Sky
Spring on the Isles of Scilly is a sight to behold.

A Splash of Colour
These harbourside properties at Mevagissey certainly look a picture with a lick of paint.

Perran Sands
It seems incredible to think that during the summer months this great reach
of sand, so peaceful now, will be packed with holidaymakers.

Opposite:
Echoes of Light
The varying degrees of wet sand reflect the colours in a sunset sky.

Rock Pool on Gwynver Beach
This pool left by the retreating tide perfectly mirrors the evening sky.

High Moors Carn
Hardy heather is the only plant able to gain a foothold
on the thin soils of the high moors.

Shetland Pony on the Lizard Head
Ponies have been introduced to the Lizard to help maintain the natural heathland.

Granite Exposed
These cliffs on the southern coast of St Mary's
on the Isles of Scilly are regularly scrubbed
clean by a ferocious ocean.

St Ives Harbour
Two scenes that show how the character and atmosphere
of this popular resort can subtly change throughout the day.

St Ives at Dusk

Evening Refrain
At day's end the dying rays reveal the inlet to Boscastle harbour.

Departure Point to the Mount
The water taxi has just left from the jetty and is the only
way of getting to and from the Mount at high tide.

The Eden Project
There are so many aspects of this phenomenally successful venture that a photographer could spend a lifetime here and still leave disappointed at being unable to cover every possible angle.

Eden by Night

Rainbow at Porthcurno
The sunlight catches rain clouds quite beautifully here
to create all the dynamics of a double rainbow.

The Back, Sennen Cove
This moment captures just why these breakwaters were built; even in the roughest seas they are a save haven for launching boats.

Early Departure
A fishing boat clears Banjo Pier at Looe.

Ancient fortress
At one time the mighty walls flanking the entrance to Chûn Castle
stood 18 feet high and would have been visible from miles around.

Falmouth Bay
Seen from high in the fields of the Roseland peninsula the
sheltered waters of the bay are a paradise for pleasure craft.

The Penwith Moors
This expanse of wilderness is probably quieter now than at any time
during the last 3000 years. Devoid of all human activity, on a still day
you can hear yourself breathe up here.

Wind Farms
Sitting just off the A30, the lofty and exposed location of these impressive structures gives them an ethereal quality, especially as they catch the afternoon sun against a thundery sky.

Wind Power
These turbines harvest the wind and provide the power for the Goonhilly Earth Station on the Lizard peninsula.

A View from Carn Galver
Engine houses of the Carn Galver mine punctuate the vista that
stretches all the way to Bosigran Castle, the headland in the distance.

Golden Ripples
A path painted by the sun leads magically to the Longships lighthouse.

Truro from the River
Mud flats of the Truro River at low tide draw the eye to the old town,
now just catching the last of the day's sunshine.

Yacht at Zone Point
The sail of the boat seems to mirror the shape of the lighthouse it is passing on this late afternoon.

Lamorna Cove
The eastern arm of the cove looks particularly shattered in appearance,
as many centuries' worth of wave slowly eat away at the tough granite.

Sand Bar Beacons
First light reveals these marker posts that warn of the presence
of the ever-shifting sands around the mouth of the River Hayle.

Seagulls on the Shoreline
Though it seems the gulls have only themselves for company, a closer
look will reveal the Godrevy lighthouse way offshore.

Last Rays of the Day
A lone holidaymaker catches the closing glory of the sun at the beach café in Sennen Cove.

Coves and Headlands
The middle distance is foreshortened by the zoom lens, giving an unusual perspective to Cape Cornwall.

Dawn over the Hayle Estuary
Caught by the sun, a line of moored boats points the way to the bustling town of Hayle.

Seagulls Alight from a Reef
This low reef in Mount's Bay is the perfect
roosting sight for seabirds come the evening.

Opposite:
Porth Nanven
Magenta sky, enhanced by the long camera exposure, is reflected on to
the rocks in this cove that sits at the end of the Cot Valley in Penwith.

Wave Rush
This day saw wave after wave batter the rocks on the north coast.

The High Tors, Bodmin
Seen from the A30, craggy hills rise impressively from the
surrounding moorland. The buildings in the foreground provide the scale.

Pasture above the Camel Estuary
The gloomy afternoon's light requires a long exposure.
Those sheep were told to keep still…

Wave Mist

Gig Rowers, Whitesands Bay
Sunday-afternoon practice – an increasingly popular sport in and around Cornwall's coastal villages.

Gigs

The *Scillonian*, anchored in the background, offloads another crowd of visitors
who flock to the islands during the World Gig Rowing Championships.

Evening On Pendeen Watch
The heath and gorse of late summer carpet gently sloping cliffs that lead to the lighthouse.

From Mullion Cove
Late afternoon and Mullion Island is silhouetted against an ominous skyline.

Pale Sun
Weak winter sun struggles to penetrate snow-laden clouds looming over the cliffs of Penwith.

Wheal Bal
A lonely relic of an industry long gone. These engine houses have come to be regarded as quintessentially Cornish.

Backlit Wave
Late sun transforms the spray into gold dust.

St Clement's Isle
This island off Mousehole claims yet another victim. The Cornish name for the village of
Mousehole is Porth Enys or Porthennis – 'port or harbour of the island'.

The Fowey Estuary
A perfect day over the estuary highlights the ancient and charming village of Fowey.

Thatched Row
This pretty line of cottages can be found on the road down to Porthoustock.

Distant lands
A ship heaves into view and helps to lead the eye to the horizon, broken by the Isles of Scilly.

High Noon in Mousehole
The midday sun in a clear sky throws colours and lines
of boats and buildings in the harbour into sharp relief.

The Escall Cliffs
Rough and weatherbeaten carns above Whitesand Bay are softened by the evening light.

Sailing on Golden Sun
This small yacht drifts in the Fal estuary, on the sunny side of the 'street'.

Dawn at Looe Bay
The drama of another day's beginning is played out in the skies over the east of Cornwall.

Opposite:
Evening Ascent
Balloons are a rare sight in Cornwall; few days are still enough to make a flight possible. This lucky aviator,
rising above the carns on Bodmin, has taken advantage of a spell of particularly calm weather.

Linnet
The female of the species, here on the Isles of Scilly, flits to and fro
during spring days, looking for suitable nesting sites in the hedgerows.

The Fowey River
Shown here in its infant stages, the river
carves its way through the hard rocks as
it runs off Bodmin Moor.

Golitha Falls
The water is turned to white silk as it cascades
over these small but beautiful falls.

The Blockhouse at Polruan
Keeping an eye on the eastern flank of the Fowey estuary this Tudor ivy-clad building proves a photogenic focal point.

Harlyn Bay
Rows of holiday caravans overlook their own private beach, softly lit in the evening summer sun.

Breakwater, Portreath
The long wall catches a succession of waves and diverts them away from the anchorage on the far side.

Low Tide in the Mount Harbour
The ancient harbour walls at St Michael's Mount
offer a rustic backdrop for this small fishing boat.

Swirling Tide
The waves play mesmerisingly around these slowly submerging rocks.

Standing Stone, Bodmin Moor
These stones, erected many of thousands of years ago, usually signal a territorial
boundary, or form part of some larger complex. Hawk's Tor looms in the distance.

St Ives Bay
Two lone clouds add interest and depth to this mid-morning sky over the bay.

Opposite:
First Light
The lichen on the rock face is the first to reflect the gloomy morning light.

De Narrow Zawn

Winter Woodlands
Fallen autumn leaves are slowly mulching down amid
moss–covered tree trunks in this wood on the edge of Bodmin.

We Shall Fight on the Beaches
The one-time first lines of defence of Britain sit high above the coves and sandy reaches of Cornwall.

Penally Hill and Beyond
A clear spring evening allows great views along the far north coast.

Patience
The heron stands as unmoving as a garden ornament,
on an inlet of the River Fal near St Just in Roseland.

The Old Wooden Pier, St Ives
The remains of this short-lived pier offer the perfect habitat for an array of tidal marine life.

Inlet on the Helford Estuary
This small craft looks a little folorn, left high and dry by the outgoing tide.

Water Falls
A long exposure gives the water a silky appearance
as it cascades over these small falls on Bodmin Moor.

St Austell Bay
The headland of Little Gribbin shines in the late sunshine.

Solitary Tree
On the relentlessly windswept Priddacombe Downs of Bodmin
trees stand little chance of growing to any great height.

Godrevy Glory
This island lighthouse creates the perfect subject at sunset.

Padstow Harbour
A battalion of hefty deep-sea trawlers crams the small harbour at Padstow.

Boscastle Dusk
The River Valency runs to the sea through
this enchanting secluded harbour village.

Across Whitesand Bay
The Cowloe reef sits mid-frame, punctuating the view to Cape Cornwall.

Coverack
A cold winter's afternoon sees this popular resort on the Lizard peninsula devoid of life.

Trevose Head Lighthouse
Sunshine follows in the wake of a passing hailstorm on this headland of the north coast.

Wave-worn
This undulating granite floor has been scoured by a trillion pebbles,
carried by a billion waves, over a million years.

Pony Trekking, St Mary's
The white sands of the Isles of Scilly give the islands a Caribbean quality.

St Michael's Mount by Night
Around Christmas time the Mount is lit up like a beacon.

Hay Bales in the Snow, Penwith

The Crown Mines, Botallack
The deep red of the oxidised ironstone is enhanced by
the unusual almost side-on angle of the light.

Low Clouds, Red Sunset
The end of the day turns these clouds a deep and brooding red.

Lizard Point
The most southerly point in Britain can also play
host to some of the roughest seas in Britain.